ACTING SHAKESPEARE
FOR AUDITIONS AND EXAMINATIONS

FRANK BARRIE

EDITED BY

JOHN NICHOLAS AND KEN PICKERING

DRAMATIC LINES, TWICKENHAM, ENGLAND
Acting Shakespeare for Auditions and Examinations
text copyright © Frank Barrie 2003

Dramatic Lines
PO Box 201
Twickenham
TW2 5RQ
England

A CIP record for this book is
available from the British Library

ISBN 1 904557 10 4

Acting Shakespeare for Auditions and Examinations
first published in 2003
by
Dramatic Lines
Twickenham England

Printed by The Dramatic Lines Press
Twickenham England

FOREWORD

This **ACTING SHAKESPEARE for Auditions and Examinations Handbook** is one of a series primarily designed to support students and teachers preparing for examinations from the Drama and Speech syllabus of Trinity College, *London.*

However, the Dramatic Lines Handbooks have much wider applications. Not only do they provide accessible and practical advice to students working towards ANY examination in Drama, Speech, Communication or Performing Arts, they also give invaluable help to those who wish to use their skills in a professional capacity as performers, teachers or communicators.

The Handbooks are quite literally something to keep to hand whenever you are working towards an important examination, performance, audition or presentation and you will find that they become your constant companions for a life in the Performance and Communications Arts.

Ken Pickering

Ken Pickering

Chief Examiner for Drama and Speech at
Trinity College, *London* and Professor of Arts Education
at the Institute for Arts in Therapy and Education

For Mary

INTRODUCTION

If you love acting and are keen to measure your talent by having a go at Shakespeare, then this is the book for you. It's an amalgam of all the advice I've been given by the many world-class actors and directors I've been lucky enough to work with whenever I've played a leading part in Shakespeare. Also included are some discoveries I've made for myself.

I've used mainly **The Oxford Shakespeare** published by the Clarendon Press in references to the text, but you won't want to go staggering around with a copy of The Complete Works, so use one of the many fine individual editions of the plays, such as **The Cambridge Pocket Shakespeare, The New Penguin Shakespeare, The Arden Shakespeare, The Warwick Shakespeare, The Signet Shakespeare** or **The Players' Shakespeare**. I've worked from all of these in various productions and have found them all to be excellent.

Good luck.

Frank Barrie

CONTENTS

WHY CHOOSE SHAKESPEARE?

He wrote marvellous parts and told wonderful stories. He moves us to laughter and tears, he sweeps us along with his great themes of love and hate, jealousy and revenge, good and evil. He has such an all embracing HUMANITY that it seems as if there is not a single thought that any of us has had or a single emotion that any of us has felt that Shakespeare didn't understand and express in the most beautiful and resonant language.

Artists' achievements are unique to themselves, they are quite different from those of scientists – if William Harvey hadn't discovered the circulation of the blood, then somebody else would have, but nobody except Shakespeare could have written:

> ………………………………...…….. *daffodils,*
> *That come before the swallow dares, and take*
> *The winds of March with beauty* ………..….…

The Winter's Tale act 4 scene 4

Shall I compare thee to a summer's day?
Thou art more lovely and more temperate.

Sonnet 18

1

But soft, what light through yonder window breaks?
It is the east, and Juliet is the sun.

Romeo and Juliet act 2 scene 1

.... We are such stuff
As dreams are made on, and our little life
Is rounded with a sleep.

The Tempest act 4 scene 1

Nothing is more breathtaking than Shakespeare at his best and no other playwright in the history of the world can touch him. The world recognises this for there's hardly a country where he has not been performed, and continues to be. He speaks to all of us. Even those who have never seen his plays, unknowingly speak him. He gave us scores of phrases which we all use. They are part of our everyday speech. Here are just a few of them:

tower of strength; beggars all description; salad days; cold comfort; sound and fury; the milk of human kindness; to play fast and loose; foul play; bag and baggage; vanish into thin air; to the manner born; the more fool you; more in sorrow than in anger; cruel to be kind; one fell swoop;

2

flesh and blood; truth will out; to be in a pickle; eaten out of house and home; it's Greek to me; more sinned against than sinning; to budge an inch; too much of a good thing; seen better days; foregone conclusion; as good luck would have it; it's high time; the long and the short of it; the crack of doom; without rhyme or reason; to give the devil his due; good riddance; sent packing; dead as a doornail; laughing stock; stony hearted; blinking idiot; for goodness' sake; it's all one to me; bloody minded; the game is up.

Have you ever spoken any of those phrases? Does it surprise you that, if so, you have been speaking Shakespeare?

In the year 2000, a poll was taken by the BBC in which Shakespeare was voted 'The Man of the Millennium' – thus affirming the remarkable prophecy made 400 years earlier by Ben Jonson, Shakespeare's friend and fellow writer, when he wrote of Shakespeare:

He was not of an age, but for all time.

3

This has been proved undeniably true – so if you have chosen Shakespeare, you will be working on the very best.

BASICS

Let's assume you are working on a Shakespeare text for the first time. You will probably have seen a Shakespeare play on film or television and, hopefully, the stage. A finished product. But when you come to act him, you must start with the basics. Acting is an art, not a science, so there are no hard and fast rules, but there are basic techniques you should learn which, in turn, will give you the freedom to experiment. Let's see what Shakespeare himself said about acting. Being an actor himself, he has a lot of useful things to say.

> *As in a theatre the eyes of men,*
> *After a well-graced actor leaves the stage,*
> *Are idly bent on him that enters next,*
> *Thinking his prattle to be tedious ....*

Richard II act 5 scene 2

I imagine you'll want to be 'well-graced' and not the one who comes on and 'prattles'. What does 'well-graced' mean? What is Shakespeare looking for?

Let's turn to the instructions which **Hamlet** gives to his little band of actors. He has written a speech which he wants them to interpolate into a play they are to perform at Court. His instructions are obviously what Shakespeare wants of HIS actors. There were no Directors in Shakespeare's day – they are a comparatively modern phenomenon, but Shakespeare must surely have supervised the rehearsals of his own plays. It would be very odd if he didn't – he was a major shareholder in the Company, a leading actor and the star playwright, so it is highly unlikely that he wouldn't also have advised the actors on the parts he wrote for them and suggested the style in which they should act them.

This is what **Hamlet** says:

Speak the speech, I pray you, as I pronounced it to you - trippingly on the tongue; but if you mouth it, as many of your players do, I had as lief the town crier had spoke my lines. Nor do not saw the air too much with your hand, thus, but use all gently; for in the very torrent, tempest, and as I may say the whirlwind of your passion, you must acquire and beget a temperance that may give it smoothness. O, it offends me to the soul to hear a robustious, periwig-pated fellow tear a passion to tatters, to very rags, to split the ears of the groundlings, who for the most part are capable of nothing but inexplicable dumb shows and noise. I would have such a fellow whipped for o'erdoing Termagant. It out-Herods Herod. Pray you avoid it ….…...

Be not too tame, neither; but let your own discretion be your tutor. Suit the action to the word, the word to the action, with this special observance, that you o'erstep not the modesty of nature. For anything so overdone is from the purpose of playing, whose end, both at the first and now, was and is to hold as 'twere the mirror up to nature ………………………..

Hamlet act 3 scene 2

'Termagant' and 'Herod' were characters in Medieval Mystery Plays which were still being performed in Shakespeare's youth. They were based on Biblical subjects and acted by amateurs. The parts of clearly lent themselves to overacting.

If the above speech seems obscure to you, it may be because you are reading it rather than speaking it – so much of Shakespeare becomes clearer when spoken. Try speaking it – was it any clearer? If it is still too difficult, you may find the following paraphrase helpful:

Please act the speech in the way I spoke it to you – swiftly. If you say it without any 'feeling', as many actors do, I may as well let the town crier speak it. Don't wave your arms about; be restrained. No matter how passionately you have to act, don't be uncontrolled. I can't bear it when an overbearing actor, in a terrible wig, overdoes everything, shouting so much that he almost deafens those standing in the cheap parts of the Theatre who invariably can't understand anything except miming and noise. I would have him whipped for overacting. It's worse than watching the demon king in a hopelessly old fashioned pantomime or melodrama – please don't do it.

Don't **underact** though – but let your own taste guide you. If you gesture, make sure that it suits what you are saying. And please, especially remember that you must never do anything unnatural because the whole purpose of acting is always to portray people and situations as they really are.

You will have noticed that the first request is that the actors should speak 'trippingly on the tongue'. In other words, at a fair pace and with good articulation. Shakespeare clearly doesn't want the lines 'declaimed' or 'intoned', he wants them to sound as if the characters had just thought of them. If HE puts this first, then so must we.

WHERE TO BEGIN

No one can suddenly start speaking Shakespeare effectively with no preparation. We wouldn't expect to be able to sit down at a piano for the very first time and be able to play it without ever having practised. Neither should we expect to be able to speak Shakespeare without some vocal preparation. Ease and facility come from constant practice.

In Shakespeare, your voice is your main instrument of communication, so you must find out what you can do with it just as a pianist must find out what he can do with the keyboard. Luckily, the voice responds very quickly to vocal exercises: even a modest amount of work will yield noticeable improvement.

There are scores of vocal exercises you can practise, and perhaps already do. I will mention just a few that work for me.

Good speaking comes from vocal relaxation and that starts with relaxation of the whole body. So we will start with one or two movement exercises.

EXERCISES

1   Stand with your feet comfortably astride and lift your arms above your head, which should be held high. Then swing your arms forward and down, bending your knees and up again, straightening your knees. Breathe out during the swing down and in during the swing up. Out through the mouth and in through the nose. (If you take great gulps of air through your mouth, you will dry up your vocal cords). Repeat the above several times, making the movements fluid and easy.

2   Roll your shoulders forward and up towards your ears, pull them down from the bottom of your shoulder blades and release. Repeat as above.

3   Relax your head forwards and roll it slowly to the left, behind, to the right and to the front. Repeat, reversing the direction.

4   Stand with your feet apart in line with your shoulders, breathe in through the nose to a count of ten, exhale through the mouth to a count of ten. Repeat five times.

5   Again breathe in through the nose to a count of
    ten and exhale to a count of ten, bending slowly
    at the waist until you are bent double. From that
    position, breathe in to a count of ten, unbending
    until you are standing straight.   Repeat five
    times.

6   Do the same as 4 but add, on your exhaling, the
    letters *Z,N,A* pronounced as *ZZZ* (pushing the
    sound forward through the teeth), *N* as *ERN*
    (with the tongue resting behind the top teeth)
    and *A* as *AH* (fully opening the throat). When
    you pronounce *ERN* you should feel your nose
    vibrating   slightly,   which   develops   nasal
    resonance.

If, on completing these exercises, you feel slightly
dizzy, then you are doing them correctly. It means
that an increased amount of oxygen has entered
your lungs.

7   Now add some articulation exercises – simple
    tongue twisters like 'Peter Piper picked a peck of
    pickled pepper'; 'She sells sea shells on the sea
    shore'; 'Peggy Babcock'; 'The Leith police
    dismisseth us'; 'The tip of the tongue and the

teeth and the lips'. Say them all five times, getting gradually quicker. Now do all those silently, moving your mouth in an exaggerated fashion.

8 Now yawn (It's a good idea to yawn just before you step on stage, because it is the best and quickest way to relax all your vocal equipment – no yawning **after** you go on stage, though, in case your audience joins in).

These exercises are simple to do and will be enough to prepare you.

CHOOSING YOUR SPEECH(ES)

Shakespeare created over 850 characters and wrote 37 plays. There are exciting scenes and superb speeches in all of them, so you will have plenty to choose from.

You may wish to choose something from this book, or something you've discovered yourself in your reading. Whatever you do, it is important to select a speech which strikes some SPARK in you. It may be that there is an emotion in the speech that you understand and identify with, or you may wish to play a favourite character, but in any event, it should be something you respond to immediately.

Perhaps if at first that seems too daunting, you may find that Leon Garfield's book **Shakespeare Stories** published by Puffin Books, will ease you into your task gently. It tells the stories clearly, and incorporates many of Shakespeare's lines.

If you are preparing your audition for a drama examination, you may be required to tell the story, or part of the story, of the play from which your speech is taken, so be prepared. In any event, you MUST know the story in order to act your speech convincingly; you MUST know at what point your speech occurs and why the character is speaking it.

Romeo and Juliet act 4 scene 3

A popular choice with young female actors is the potion speech from **Romeo and Juliet,** act 4 scene 3, beginning: 'Farewell. God knows when we shall meet again.' If that is your choice, then before embarking on it, READ THE ENTIRE PLAY.

So, let us remind ourselves of the basic plot of 'Romeo and Juliet':

After a brawl between two Veronese families, the Montagues and the Capulets, the Prince of Verona threatens death to anyone who disturbs the streets again.

Montague's son, Romeo, masked, at a Capulet dance, falls instantly in love with Capulet's daughter, Juliet.

Later, in the garden, when he sees her come out onto her balcony and overhears her speaking of her love of him, he announces himself and their love scene follows. The next day, Friar Lawrence marries them in secret.

When Romeo refuses to fight with Tybalt, a Capulet, who is now Romeo's cousin by marriage, Romeo's headstrong friend, Mercutio, takes up the challenge. Mercutio is killed by mischance and the enraged Romeo kills Tybalt.

Romeo is banished from Verona by the Prince. Friar Lawrence instructs him to spend the night with Juliet and then wait in Mantua until recall is possible.

When Juliet's father insists that she must marry a young nobleman, Paris, and she gets no sympathy from her mother or her nurse, the Friar gives her an opiate that will put her in a death-like trance for 42 hours. She will be left as if for dead in the Capulet tomb and when she wakes, Romeo will be there.

Juliet is laid in the tomb, but the Friar's message to Romeo miscarries and Romeo only hears that Juliet is dead. Romeo rushes to the tomb and is surprised by Paris, whom he kills. He then drinks poison and dies by Juliet's side. Juliet wakes as the Friar enters and, seeing Romeo dead, stabs herself.

The Prince and the heads of the families are roused. Montague and Capulet are reconciled over the bodies of their children.

Those are the bare bones of the story which Shakespeare fleshes out with some of the most beautiful poetry ever written.

The action immediately before the 'potion' speech:

Juliet has been given the opiate by **Friar Lawrence** and has pretended to agree to marry **Paris**. She dismisses the nurse, who leaves the stage with Juliet's mother. Now she is alone.

Imagine her state of mind.

- Imagine what it would be like to have secretly married a young man you are desperately in love with, whose family you know your parents hate.

- Imagine that your new husband has killed a man who is a member of your family and is exiled for it.

- Imagine that your father then insists that you must marry someone else who you do not know.

You are desperate and seek the advice of your priest. Your priest has a wild plan that, by taking a drug, you will appear to be dead, be placed in your tomb, that somehow **Romeo** will come and find you when you awake and SOMEHOW everything will work out well. You would have doubts, wouldn't you? So does **Juliet**.

Remember that she is only 13 years old (she would have been 14 on Lammas Eve, soon after her death) and the situation is overwhelming for her, but she is a bright, intelligent and passionate girl of great courage. She decides she must act on the Friar's advice. Here, (act 4 scene 3, line 14), she speaks:

Farewell. God knows when we shall meet again.
I have a faint cold fear thrills through my veins
That almost freezes up the heat of life.
I'll call them back again to comfort me.
Nurse! – What should she do here?
My dismal scene I needs must act alone.
Come, vial.

What if this mixture do not work at all?
Shall I be married then tomorrow morning?
This shall forbid it. Lie thou there.
What if it be a poison which the Friar
Subtly hath ministered to have me dead,
Lest in this marriage he should be dishonoured
Because he married me before to Romeo?
I fear it is – and yet methinks it should not,
For he hath still been tried a holy man.
How if, when I am laid into the tomb,
I wake before the time that Romeo
Come to redeem me? There's a fearful point!
Shall I not then be stifled in the vault,
To whose foul mouth no healthsome air breathes in,
And there die strangled ere my Romeo comes?
Or, if I live, is it not very like
The horrible conceit of death and night,
Together with the terror of the place –
As in a vault, an ancient receptacle
Where for this many hundred years the bones
Of all my buried ancestors are packed;
Where bloody Tybalt, yet but green in earth,
Lies fest'ring in his shroud; where, as they say,
At some hours in the night spirits resort –
Alack, alack, is it not like that I,
So early waking – what with loathsome smells,

And shrieks like mandrakes torn out of the earth,
That living mortals, hearing them, run mad –
O, if I wake, shall I not be distraught,
Environed with all these hideous fears,
And madly play with my forefathers' joints,
And pluck the mangled Tybalt from his shroud,
And, in this rage, with some great kinsman's bone
As with a club dash out my desp'rate brains?
O, look! Methinks I see my cousin's ghost
Seeking out Romeo that did spit his body
Upon a rapier's point. Stay, Tybalt, stay!
Romeo, I come! This do I drink to thee.

In performance, this speech can easily be ruined if the actor is too hysterical and 'tears a passion to tatters', as **Hamlet** says. There are clear indications where hysteria takes over, but the actor must always be in control. If not, the speech will become incoherent – the words will be lost in a welter of emotion.

A young actor once said to me after she had performed this speech, 'There are too many words – they get in the way of my emotions'. If ever YOU feel like that, then you will know that you have gone astray.

Her dilemma was the result of the enjoyment she'd derived from improvisations. Improvisation is fun, it can stimulate your imagination and release your inhibitions, but remember it is only an exercise, a stage on your journey, it's not your destination and certainly not a substitute for the kind of work you need to do when rehearsing Shakespeare. It mustn't replace illuminating the words: it's the words which matter most. The emotions you feel as an actor must be expressed through the words. The words ARE **Juliet**.

Now let's look at the speech in detail and think about how it might be staged.

Farewell. God knows when we shall meet again.

Juliet is in her bedroom and she is replying to her mother's exit line 'Good night, get thee to bed and rest, for thou hast need'. **Juliet** might smile and say, 'Farewell', quite cheerfully to her mother, because she is pretending that she is happy to be marrying **Paris**.

A cheerful beginning will give a good contrast to the rest of the speech. The rest of the line should be spoken a beat after 'Farewell', to allow for her mother's exit and it should be spoken to herself, or to the audience, with foreboding. This will give a believable bridge to the following lines.

> *I have a faint cold fear thrills through my veins*
> *That almost freezes up the heat of life.*

Feel the cold fear slightly before the line – you might cross your arms and hold yourself as you speak.

> *I'll call them back again to comfort me.*
> *Nurse!*

Here you might rush to where your mother and the nurse have exited – don't be too loud on 'Nurse!' – you don't actually want her to respond.

> *………….. What should she do here?*
> *My dismal scene I needs must act alone.*

'What should she do here' means what would be the point of her being here. 'My dismal scene I needs must act alone' enlists the audience's sympathy for the young actor playing the part and stresses **Juliet's** courage.

Now return to centre stage – the best place to 'act a scene' – and summon up your courage on the next line.

Come, vial.

This short line indicates a pause for action – in this case the finding of the small container which you might perhaps have in a pocket in your practice skirt. You will be wearing a long skirt, won't you? If you have difficulty finding the vial, don't panic – take natural time – **Juliet** might have had difficulty too. Open the vial (I've seen actors forget to do this) and lift it towards your mouth. Then suddenly arrest the movement as the next thought occurs to you.

What if this mixture do not work at all?
Shall I be married then tomorrow morning?

Be rational in this statement and in full control.

This shall forbid it. Lie thou there.

Juliet is referring to a dagger, which you might wear tucked into your waistband. She puts it on the 'bed'. In an audition situation, it is practically certain that a bed will not be at your disposal. You will have to make do with a chair, or preferably two, which you will have arranged side by side before you begin the speech. If there is only one chair available, don't let that worry you – the person taking the audition will understand your problem and will admire you for dealing with it without fussing. If there are two chairs, you might sit on one. If there is only one, keep standing – you can't sit on your dagger.

Think of these practical problems before the audition and decide on what you must do in particular circumstances.

Now look at the vial.

> *What if it be a poison which the Friar*
> *Subtly hath ministered to have me dead,*
> *Lest in this marriage he should be dishonoured*
> *Because he married me before to Romeo?*

This should be spoken all on one breath and swiftly – carry the thought through.

> *I fear it is – and yet methinks it should not,*
> *For he hath still been tried a holy man.*

SAYING the word 'fear' means that you don't have to ACT fear – the word does it for you. Move swiftly on – her mind is agile.

'Methinks' is pronounced m'thinks (*ie* with a very short 'e' – NOT 'Mee' thinks). 'Still' means always and 'tried' means proved.

> *How if, when I am laid into the tomb,*
> *I wake before the time that Romeo*
> *Come to redeem me? There's a fearful point!*

This is a sudden thought – again speak the lines on one breath.

'Redeem' means reclaim and 'There's a fearful point' means that's a frightening possibility – not, as I witnessed once, a reference to the dagger.

> *Shall I not then be stifled in the vault,*
> *To whose foul mouth no healthsome air breathes in,*
> *And there die strangled ere my Romeo comes?*

All on one breath and not TOO terrified. There's much more of that to come.

'Strangled' means suffocated.

Or, if I live, is it not very like
The horrible conceit of death and night,
Together with the terror of the place –
As in a vault, an ancient receptacle
Where for this many hundred years the bones
Of all my buried ancestors are packed;
Where bloody Tybalt, yet but green in earth,
Lies fest'ring in his shroud; where, as they say,
At some hours in the night spirits resort –
Alack, alack, is it not like that I,
So early waking – what with loathsome smells,
And shrieks like mandrakes torn out of the earth,
That living mortals, hearing them, run mad –
O, if I wake, shall I not be distraught,
Environed with all these hideous fears,
And madly play with my forefathers' joints,
And pluck the mangled Tybalt from his shroud,
And, in this rage, with some great kinsman's bone
As with a club dash out my desp'rate brains?

This is the hardest section of the speech – it's all one sentence and the momentum must be kept up. Start fairly slowly so you've plenty of time to build to a climax. Use upward inflections as much as you can, especially at the ends of lines – this will help to give a buoyancy and drive to the speech. Work out exactly where you are going to take breaths. It's a long, tumbling sentence where each nightmare image gives way to another even more terrible, but however swiftly you eventually speak and however terrified you become, never lose the clarity of the words.

'Like' means likely, 'conceit' means picture or image and 'environed' means surrounded. **Tybalt** is 'bloody' from **Romeo's** sword, 'green in earth' means newly buried and also suggest the colour of festering. 'Mandrakes' were plants whose forked roots resembled the shape of a man. They were believed to shriek when uprooted and so drive the listener mad.

> *O, look! Methinks I see my cousin's ghost*
> *Seeking out Romeo that did spit his body*
> *Upon a rapier's point. Stay, Tybalt, stay!*

You will have reached a high level of panic in the previous section, so change the tone slightly here and let the panic give way to the shock of the vision of **Tybalt** which you should see downstage, left or right, so we can still see your face. You might lift your hand towards the image, the palm trying to block the image out.

'Spit' means pierced like a joint of meat on a cooking spit, 'stay' means stop.

You might make 'Stay, Tybalt, stay!' the climax of your speech – it might be the loudest you become.

Romeo, I come! This do I drink to thee.

This is a confident resolution AND a declaration of love. It's not everyday speech, it's grand and romantic, but it must be sincerely felt.

Kneel on 'This do I drink to thee', so you are half way to collapsing on the floor. Don't collapse suddenly – the opiate needs time to work – and DON'T act as if you are poisoned – it's a sleeping draught. Exhale as you lie down and at the end don't snap out of your acting suddenly – let the emotion stay with you for a little while. If you recover too quickly, you will seem insincere.

COMMON FAULTS

The advice I have offered on **Juliet's** speech, has implications for all the monologues I have chosen in this book. But before we go on to discuss them, it may be helpful to mention the most common faults which I have noticed in the many hundreds of auditions I have encountered.

1   A desperate anxiety to impress. If you are playing only one speech, or one short scene, you can't convey the whole part, nor should you try to. If you are playing **Lady Macbeth**, you can't put five acts of vaulting ambition into a few lines. If you try to, then you will not appear to be human. Play the detail of the speech, not the generality. You are playing **Lady Macbeth** at a particular point in the story, so concentrate on that. The best **Lady Macbeth** I have seen was Judi Dench. She approached the part in a totally original way, but she didn't act in a way which wasn't fully justified by the lines. We have become used to implacable **Lady Macbeths** who terrify us with their evil, but Dame Judi discovered the vulnerability of the character implicit in the lines and played that. When she spoke the famous incantation from act 1 scene 5:

.... Come, you spirits
That tend on mortal thoughts, unsex me here,
And fill me from the crown to the top top-full
Of direst cruelty. Make thick my blood,
Stop up th'acess and passage to remorse,
That no compunctious visitings of nature
Shake my fell purpose, nor keep peace between
Th'effect and it. Come to my woman's breasts,
And take my milk for gall, you murd'ring ministers,
Wherever in your sightless substances
You wait on nature's mischief. Come, thick night,
And pall thee in the dunnest smoke of hell,
That my keen knife see not the wound it makes,
Nor heaven peep through the blanket of the dark
To cry 'Hold, hold!'

she gave the impression that she was *asking* the spirits to help her, not *commanding* them. She was restrained, a believable human being. She examined the text and related to what was human in it, she didn't add to it, she obeyed Shakespeare's instructions – she was *temperate.* Don't attempt to impress, attempt to be truthful and simple – this will impress far more than histrionic displays. Remember those words **truthful** and **simple**. Shakespeare will do the rest for you.

2   Don't think you will be more interesting if you move around a lot and wave your arms about. You won't, you will just look restless. If there's no good reason to move, stand still and use gesture only when you need to.

3   Don't put on a special 'poetry voice', just speak clearly. Observe the rhythms of the verse, but don't let them dominate. Go for *sense* rather than *sound.* If you get the sense right, then the sound will take care of itself.

4   Don't 'colour wash' the whole speech in one mood or emotion: respond to the individual phrases. Shakespeare's lines work on emotions and these can change within a single line. Observe these changes, allow yourself to feel the emotional variations and the speech will come to life.

5   Don't confuse whispering with sincerity. Always be easy to hear. There's not much point in learning the lines if you keep them to yourself.

Remember that a general audience is hearing the words for perhaps the first time, so it is essential that they are **clearly audible**. Don't make your audience **strain** to hear, they may decide not to bother.

Hamlet says 'Let's go hear a play'. He doesn't say 'Let's go *try* to hear a play'.

THE SEVEN Ws

When thinking about your character, you might find it useful to ask yourself seven questions, which I shall call the Seven Ws.

Who am I?

How do I appear outwardly and what am I inwardly? What has happened in my life to make me what I am?

Where am I?

In my bedroom? On the street? In a wood? A banqueting hall? The stage? (You'll feel different according to the location).

When is it?

I will be conditioned by the period in which I live, even by the clothes I wear. What do the clothes tell me about how I should move?

What do I want?

If you are not sure, invent something which only you know. (It will give depth to your performance – it's your secret.)

What obstacles do I have to overcome to achieve my aims?

Someone's hatred? Someone's incompetence? My own doubts?

What effect do I want to make?

Appear vulnerable? Strong? Terrified? Terrifying? Charming?

Who am I talking to?

My best friend? My enemy? My lover? My mother? The King? An assassin? God? Myself? The audience? (Your manner would be different towards each of them).

When you have answers to all these questions, you will have a much greater sense of the reality of your character.

CONFIDENCE

Acting is 90% confidence. Not arrogance, **confidence** – the confidence which comes from thorough preparation.

I know that confidence can slip away alarmingly in a performance situation, especially if you get a reaction you weren't expecting – or no reaction at all when you WERE expecting it (particularly dispiriting in comedy). Anxiety can step in and you can become too 'effortful'.

Remember that your audience wants to believe in what you're doing and they can only do that if you believe in it too. If you feel yourself becoming over anxious and trying too hard, pull yourself back. Be truthful, be measured, be controlled. Mean what you say. If there was ever one phrase that defined good acting it is that – **Mean what you say.**

Now let us go on to explore some more speeches. If you choose to perform one or other of them, time them carefully to make sure they are no longer than the time allotted to you in the audition.

ANTONY

Julius Caesar act 3 scene 1

Mark Antony is a highly theatrical part: he is eloquent and opportunistic, calculating and bold.

His speech in the Forum: 'Friends, Romans, countrymen lend me your ears', is the most famous speech in the play – a masterly blend of emotional appeal and blistering irony which achieves its expected result.

However, I would not recommend it for audition purposes, not solely because it is so familiar, but because it really needs some reaction from the mob to achieve its full effect.

A wiser choice would be the soliloquy he speaks over the dead body of **Caesar**. It is just as eloquent as the Forum speech, but it is wholly and sincerely felt and has an extraordinary power.

> *O pardon me, thou bleeding piece of earth,*
> *That I am meek and gentle with these butchers.*
> *Thou art the ruins of the noblest man*
> *That ever lived in the tide of times.*
> *Woe to the hand that shed this costly blood!*

Over thy wounds now do I prophesy –
Which like dumb mouths do ope their ruby lips
To beg the voice and utterance of my tongue –
A curse shall light upon the limbs of men;
Domestic fury and fierce civil strife
Shall cumber all the parts of Italy;
Blood and destruction shall be so in use,
And dreadful objects so familiar,
That mothers shall but smile when they behold
Their infants quartered with the hands of war,
All pity choked with custom of fell deeds;
And Caesar's spirit, ranging for revenge,
With Ate by his side come hot from hell,
Shall in these confines with a monarch's voice
Cry 'havoc!' and let slip the dogs of war,
That this foul deed shall smell above the earth
With carrion men, groaning for burial.

The action immediately before the 'Forum' speech:

Prior to this speech, Caesar has been stabbed to death and his friend Antony, as a political manoeuvre, has pretended to the assassins that he sympathises with their motives. He's even shaken hands with them and has agreed that he will not blame them for the murder when he speaks to the crowd in the Forum. He is filled with supressed rage and grief, mingled with a certain amount of self-disgust at his own dissembling.

He kneels over Caesar's body.

O pardon me, thou bleeding piece of earth,
That I am meek and gentle with these butchers.

The first short word 'O' is a wonderful opportunity for the actor – lengthen it, speak it with deep feeling, almost gruffly and HATE the words 'meek and gentle' – colour them with self-disgust – and stress the word 'butchers'. He hates them even more.

Change the tone on

Thou art the ruins of the noblest man
That ever lived in the tide of times.

Speak it simply and sincerely as a prelude to the re-energised

Woe to the hand that shed this costly blood!

The rest of the speech is a relentless, terrifying account of the horrors to come and needs to be acted with contained anger, rising to a climax on

Cry 'havoc!' and let slip the dogs of war.

The actor might rise on the previous line 'Come hot from hell' as the incarnation of revenge springing from the earth and stand, four-square, legs apart, arms half raised, fists clenched, looking upwards – a physical image as powerful as his words.

Stress the consonants throughout, speak as forcefully as the rage within him and increase the pace from 'And Caesar's spirit' to the end.

This speech, which **Antony** begins as a prophesy, quickly transforms into a curse and should have all the force which that implies.

The language is largely accessible – 'dumb mouths' is frequently used by Shakespeare as an image for wounds, particularly those which can accuse. 'Cumber' means burden, 'quartered' means hacked to pieces, 'with custom of foul deeds' means because of the commonness of cruel actions, and 'ranging' means roving in search of prey. 'Ate' (pronounced Artay), is the goddess of strife and discord. 'Confines' (accent on the second syllable) means regions, 'carrion men' means corpses.

ISABELLA

Measure for Measure act 2 scene 4

To whom should I complain? Did I tell this,
Who would believe me? O perilous mouths,
That bear in them one and the selfsame tongue
Either of condemnation or approof,
Bidding the law make curtsy to their will,
Hooking both right and wrong to th'appetite,
To follow as it draws! I'll to my brother.
Though he hath fall'n by prompture of the blood,
Yet hath he in him such a mind of honour
That had he twenty heads to tender down
On twenty bloody blocks, he'd yield them up
Before his sister should her body stoop
To such abhorred pollution.
Then Isabel live chaste, and brother die:
More than our brother is our chastity.
I'll tell him yet of Angelo's request,
And fit his mind to death, for his soul's rest.

Isabella, a novitiate nun, is a very problematic character to play. Usually a modern audience sympathises with her predicament but is shocked by how she proposes to deal with it.

The eventual 'happy ending', when she is married off

to the **Duke of Vienna**, is particularly difficult for the actor. Shakespeare senses this, for she falls strangely silent. The above speech, however, is very effective and also quite brief, so it's a good audition piece to prepare if your allotted time is fairly short.

The background is this:

Angelo, recognised throughout Vienna as a cold, passionless, prig ('a man whose blood is very snow-broth') has been left in charge of the city expressly to stamp out sexual licence. In the process he has imprisoned Isabella's brother Claudio and condemned him to death for fornication.

Isabella has come to Angelo to plead for her brother's life and to her horror, Angelo proposes that only if she agrees to sleep with him will he release Claudio. She can hardly encompass this level of hypocrisy. It is as if everything she thought true is false and hollow – 'seeming, seeming!'

In her confusion, she clings to her religious belief that if she loses her chastity, then not only will she be cast out from the Kingdom of Heaven, but that Claudio too would be damned if his life were saved by such means.

The speech then must be acted with blazing sincerity. Stand still, like a pillar of rectitude. Any moves would diminish her strength of feeling. 'I'll to my brother' implies movement, but it is more effective to wait until the end of the speech. Mental turmoil is often better conveyed through utter stillness as it allows us to concentrate solely on the words. Perhaps she might clasp her hands and hold them to her bosom to remind us of her calling.

She is debating within herself here, not talking to the audience. To talk directly to them would externalise her confusion and dissipate it.

The first one and a half lines are filled with astonishment.

> *To whom should I complain? Did I tell this,*
> *Who would believe me?*

The next six, which form a single sentence, are filled

with disgust and should be driven along fairly swiftly.

> *O perilous mouths,*
> *That bear in them one and the selfsame tongue*
> *Either of condemnation or approof,*
> *Bidding the law make curtsy to their will,*
> *Hooking both right and wrong to th'appetite,*
> *To follow as it draws!*

On

> *I'll to my brother.*

she gains confidence, inspired by her conviction that **Claudio** will never doubt her decision, so again, drive the speech on – though perhaps you might pull back slightly after

> *……. and brother die:*

as she realises the implications for him. She might close her eyes on

> *More than our brother is our chastity.*

as if clinging to a religious text. She may also find

some peace in contemplating her brother's 'soul's rest', so it would be logical to put a great deal of emphasis on those last two words.

'Prompture of the blood' means sexual desire and 'bloody blocks' are execution blocks.

LAUNCE

The Two Gentlemen of Verona act 4 scene 4

Launce enters with his dog Crab.

When a man's servant shall play the cur with him, look you, it goes hard. One that I brought up of a puppy, one that I saved from drowning when three or four of his blind brothers and sisters went to it. I have taught him, even as one would say precisely 'Thus I would teach a dog'. I was sent to deliver him as a present to Mistress Silvia from my master, and I came no sooner into the dining-chamber but he steps me to her trencher and steals her capon's leg. O, 'tis a foul thing when a cur cannot keep himself in all companies. I would have, as one should say, one that takes upon him to be a dog indeed, to be, as it were, a dog at all things. If I had not had more wit than he, to take a fault upon me that he did, I think verily he had been hanged for't. Sure as I live, he had suffered for't. You shall judge. He thrusts me himself into the company of three or four gentleman-like dogs under the Duke's table. He had not been there – bless the mark – a pissing-while but all the chamber smelled him. 'Out with the dog,' says one. 'What cur is that?' says another. 'Whip him out,' says a third. 'Hang him up,' says the Duke. I, having been acquainted with the smell before, knew it was Crab, and goes me to the fellow that whips the dogs. 'Friend,' quoth I, 'you mean to whip the dog.' 'Ay, marry do I,' quoth he. 'You do him the more wrong,' quoth I, ''twas I did the thing you wot of.' He makes me no more ado, but whips me out of the chamber. How many masters would do this for his servant? Nay, I'll be sworn I have sat in the stocks for puddings he hath stolen, otherwise he had been executed. I have stood on the pillory for geese he hath killed, otherwise he had suffered for't. (To Crab) *Thou think'st not of this now. Nay, I remember the trick you served me when I took my leave of Madam Silvia. Did not I bid thee still mark me, and do as I do? When didst thou see me heave up my leg and make water against a gentlewoman's farthingale? Didst thou ever see me do such a trick?*

This is a very funny and endearing speech, which depends a great deal on the personality of the performer – not to mention the dog. A real dog would not be welcome at an audition, unfortunately, but there's plenty of humour to be had from a totally impassive toy dog, so try to find one as lifelike as possible. A down-at-heel, old mongrel type would be best.

Launce's loyal defence of his dog is the bedrock of this speech, so don't go solely for laughs – go for warmth of feeling. You might tuck him under your arm affectionately, or you might sit down beside him and give him the occasional stroke.

Launce is **Proteus**' servant, he's one of the long-suffering, stoic, working-class who accept their lot and make the best of things. Find some regional accent which you are comfortable with and if you have an off-beat appearance, slightly dishevelled, so much the better.

Play the speech with ease and take your time – it's a comic interlude and doesn't need to be delivered 'trippingly on the tongue'. You must be very much at home with your audience – when you are not looking at your dog, look at them. Don't be afraid of the vulgarity – be bold and lift your leg like a dog when describing Crab's behaviour with **Madam Silvia**.

When you get your laughs, you might fill in the gaps by tickling Crab under the chin – anything to establish ease and affection.

Not many moves here – do what a comedian does – come down front, centre stage and stay there.

A 'trencher' is a wooden plate, a 'capon' is a castrated cockerel fattened for eating and a 'farthingale' is a hooped petticoat. 'Quoth' means said.

BEATRICE

Much Ado About Nothing act 3 scene 1

When **Beatrice** was born 'a star danced' and, as she says, 'under that was I born'. She's a warm, witty woman, bright as a button. She's also a confirmed spinster, engaged in a 'merry war' with a confirmed bachelor, the big-hearted but seemingly cynical, **Benedick**.

These two are clearly meant for each other, but they don't seem to know it. So their friends decide to help the process along by 'setting them up'. **Benedick's** male friends make sure he overhears them talking about **Beatrice's** supposed love for him. This works a treat and in a very funny prose soliloquy, we see that **Benedick** has fallen for it when he says, 'Love me? Why, it must be requited .... When I said I would die a bachelor, I did not think I would live 'til I were married'.

Next, **Beatrice's** female friends play the same trick on her. When they have gone, we wait eagerly for **Beatrice's** reaction.

What fire is in mine ears? Can this be true?
Stand I condemned for pride and scorn so much?

Contempt, farewell; and maiden pride, adieu.
No glory lives behind the back of such.
And, Benedick, love on. I will requite thee,
Taming my wild heart to thy loving hand.
If thou dost love, my kindness shall incite thee
To bind our loves up in a holy band.
For others say thou dost deserve, and I
Believe it better than reportingly.

Notice that there is none of the broad humour of **Benedick's** reaction here. **Beatrice's** speech is touching and sincere. She accepts the criticisms of herself with humility, vows to reform, to love **Benedick** unconditionally and to waste no time in marrying him. ('my kindness shall incite thee to bind our loves up in a holy band').

The speech is not just a rush of excitement and happiness – there are nuances within it – but generally act it as if you are lit up with the fire of love. It is very elegantly written – ten lines of exquisite rhyming verse, the only instance of its kind in the play – and it must be elegantly acted. The formality of the verse is a wonderful counterpoint to the depth of the feeling expressed – it gives it dignity.

What fire is in my ears? Can this be true?

The first line is excited, but puzzled, followed by the humility of

Stand I condemned for pride and scorn SO MUCH?

Which leads to the joyful release of

.... **Benedick**, *love on.*

Smile broadly here, as if speaking directly to him. Allow yourself a moment of vulnerability on

IF thou dost love,

Before the return to full confidence on

...... I BELIEVE it – better than reportingly.

Make us feel happy for you by sharing your feelings with us.

'Adieu' (goodbye) is pronounced 'Adew' – it always is in Shakespeare. In this instance the rhyme with 'true' makes that clear.

This speech is a splendid choice if your allotted time is very short. In any event, it's always better to be a little too short than far too long.

RICHARD

Richard III act 5 scene 5

(It may be scene 3 in your edition)

Give me another horse! Bind up my wounds!

Have mercy, Jesu! Soft, I did but dream.

O coward conscience, how dost thou afflict me?

The lights burn blue. It is now dead midnight.

Cold fearful drops stand on my trembling flesh.

What do I fear? Myself? There's none else by.

Richard loves Richard; that is, I am I.

Is there a murderer here? No. Yes, I am.

Then fly! What, from myself? Great reason. Why?

Lest I revenge. Myself upon myself?

Alack, I love myself. Wherefore? For any good

That I myself have done unto myself?

O no, alas, I rather hate myself

For hateful deeds committed by myself.

I am a villain. Yet I lie: I am not.

Fool, of thyself speak well. – Fool, do not flatter.

My conscience hath a thousand several tongues,

And every tongue brings in a several tale,

And every tale condemns me for a villain.

Perjury, perjury, in the high'st degree!

Murder, stern murder, in the direst degree!

All several sins, all used in each degree,

Throng to the bar, crying all, 'Guilty, guilty!'

I shall despair. There is no creature loves me,

And if I die no soul will pity me.
Nay, wherefore should they? – Since that I myself
Find in myself no pity to myself.
Methought the souls of all that I had murdered
Came to my tent, and every one did threat
Tomorrow's vengeance on the head of Richard.

Richard is having a nightmare, so the opportunities for the actor are enormous. Nightmares are terrifying because we see and feel horror on a scale rarely encountered in real life – so there is every reason here for big, bold acting.

Until this point in the play we have seen little vulnerability in **Richard**. The 'bottled spider' has dispatched his enemies with awesome facility and his rise to power has been breathtakingly swift and sure.

Now he discovers a conscience ('thus conscience doth make cowards of us all' – **Hamlet**) and for just a few moments we wonder if he is going to reveal a more tender side to his nature. Not for long though. There is no conversion and he is soon back on track.

It's a wonderful part to play and it has made instant stars of many actors who have played him throughout the ages. Richard Burbage was the first – Shakespeare wrote it for him – and Burbage grabbed his opportunities with both hands. His success was so great that for a time he was referred to in real life as Richard the Third, rather like those actors in Soap Operas who convince the public that they really are the characters they play.

Here's a contemporary funny story about this:

Upon a time when Burbage played Richard III, there was a citizen gone so far in liking with him, that before she went from the play, she appointed him to come that night unto her by the name of Richard the Third. William Shakespeare, overhearing their conclusion, went before, was entertained and at his game ere Burbage came. Then message being brought that Richard the Third was at the door, Shakespeare caused return to be made that William the Conqueror was before Richard the Third.

It is his wit, energy and fighting spirit which are so mesmerising and attractive in **Richard**. So, a rattling good part then and one which you can go to town on – in every sense.

You will probably know that Shakespeare's **Richard** is hump-backed – warped in body as well as mind – so give some indication of that in the way you hold your shoulders. He also had a withered arm, so hold your arm like a claw – it's practically useless. As he tells us defiantly, in the world famous first speech of the play, he is 'deformed, unfinished, ... scarce half made up, and that so lamely and unfashionable that dogs bark at me as I halt by them'.

All this is fascinating in itself. Add to it the fantastically energetic lines which Shakespeare gives him and you have a stunning role.

Do you know why they are called 'roles'?

It's because each actor in Shakespeare's day was given only his individual part – he didn't get the whole script because it all had to be hand-written. (Think of the labour involved.) So he only got his own part with the 'cues' – a line or two of other people's speeches – to tell him when to speak. They were written on rolls of paper – hence 'roles'. You could tell immediately how big your role was – by the size of the roll. Burbage's roll must have caused some envious glances when it was handed out.

Back to the speech. **Richard** is in his tent which is pitched near the battlefield at Bosworth and he has been visited by the ghosts of some of the people he's murdered.

Lie asleep on the floor at the beginning – a foetal position, awkwardly held, is effective. Burst out of it with your first words – don't wake slowly – it's a sudden burst of energy.

> *Give me another horse! Bind up my wounds!*
> *Have mercy, Jesu!*

– the exclamation marks tell you what to do.

The first phrase is prophetic – he loses his horse in the battle and utters the famous cry, 'A horse! A horse! My kingdom for a horse!'

Despise the word 'coward' in the line following – cowardice is one of the few vices which is totally alien to him.

O coward conscience, how dost thou afflict me?

'The lights burn blue' is alarming to him. Shakespeare's original audience would know, with **Richard**, that when a candle burns blue it means that ghosts are abroad.

Be astonished that 'cold fearful drops' (of sweat) stand on your trembling flesh. Wipe your forehead with your hands and look at your fingers – you've never known that before.

The crisp, short phrases which follow should be acted energetically and swiftly – it's like an argument between two people. Don't pause for thought – **Richard** has one of the most agile minds in all literature.

> *What do I fear? Myself? There's none else by.*
> *Richard loves Richard; that is, I am I.*
> *Is there a murderer here? No. Yes, I am.*
> *Then fly! What, from myself? Great reason. Why?*
> *Lest I revenge. Myself upon myself?*
> *Alack, I love myself. Wherefore? For any good*
> *That I myself have done unto myself?*

You might pause slightly after

O no, ...

but plunge straight on afterwards. On

I am a villain, yet I lie, I am not.
Fool of thyself speak well. – Fool do not flatter.

you might imagine a demon on either shoulder and address them directly, moving your head from side to side like a ventriloquist's doll. Again, no pauses.

The next passage, from 'My conscience .....' through to 'Guilty, guilty!' should be driven through like a galloping horse – you've got to have plenty of breath at your disposal, so take a great gulp before you start. Take the pitch up a notch on each line and speak as many lines as you possibly can on one breath. If you have to take another breath, take it after '..... in the high'st degree!' and reach a ringing climax on 'Guilty, guilty!' Lengthen the last syllables of these words and imagine them echoing around a huge Courtroom – make them reverberate.

After this, a complete change of tone – clipped and detached. No self-pity please on

> *….. There is no creature loves me,*
> *And if I die no soul will pity me.*
> *Nay, wherefore should they? – Since that I myself*
> *Find in myself no pity to myself.*

– he's entirely matter of fact. On

> *Methought the souls of all that I had murdered*
> *Came to my tent, and every one did threat*
> *Tomorrow's vengeance on the head of Richard.*

let's see you getting an inkling that you may lose the battle tomorrow, but again, NO SELF-PITY.

You might begin to rise from your crouching position to be standing for 'Guilty, guilty!', but otherwise, no dashing about – it's concentrated stuff. And it's wonderful.

VIOLA

Twelfth Night act 2 scene 2

Viola (accent on the first syllable – not like the musical instrument), is one of Shakespeare's most appealing and sympathetic heroines. She is a kind, brave and generous girl, who has known great sadness – the supposed drowning of her twin brother **Sebastian** - AND great danger.

The background is this:

Viola has been shipwrecked, penniless in a foreign land, but instead of feeling sorry for herself, she makes the best of things, disguises herself as a boy, calls herself Cesario and gets a job – as page to the Count Orsino. She soon falls in love with him, but can't declare her love (a) because he thinks she is a boy and (b) because Orsino is extravagantly in love with Olivia, a neighbouring Countess. Olivia does not return his love, so Orsino sends Viola/Cesario to Olivia to woo her on his behalf.

In spite of her feelings, Viola performs this task to the best of her ability. Olivia rejects the message, but is instantly attracted to the messenger, not realising that Cesario is in fact a girl.

When Cesario/Viola leaves, Olivia longs for 'him' to return the next day so sends her steward Malvolio running after him to say so. She also tells him to give back a ring which she says Cesario has given her. No ring WAS given, but Viola is too honourable a girl to expose Olivia in a lie, so says 'She took the ring of me, I'll none of it'. Malvolio, exasperated, throws it on the ground and exits.

At this point the speech begins.

I left no ring with her. What means this lady?
Fortune forbid my outside have not charmed her.
That straight methought her eyes had lost her tongue,
For she did speak in starts, distractedly.
She loves me, sure. The cunning of her passion
Invites me in this churlish messenger.
None of my lord's ring! Why, he sent her none.
I am the man. If it be so – as 'tis –
Poor lady, she were better love a dream!
Disguise, I see thou art a wickedness
Wherein the pregnant enemy does much.
How easy is it for the proper-false

In women's waxen hearts to set their forms!
Alas, our frailty is the cause, not we,
For such as we are made of, such we be.
How will this fadge? My master loves her dearly,
And I, poor monster, fond as much on him,
And she, mistaken, seems to dote on me.
What will become of this? As I am man,
My state is desperate for my master's love.
As I am woman, now, alas the day,
What thriftless sighs shall poor Olivia breathe!
O time, thou must untangle this, not I.
It is too hard a knot for me t'untie.

Each section of this speech reveals a different aspect of **Viola's** character. Her kindness, sensitivity, humour and commonsense, all come into play. I've seen it performed many times and it works best when the actor really allows herself to THINK her way through it. So let the audience come to you – don't over project.

The worst performance I've seen was from an actor who played it angrily – even crossly shouting the first line to the exiting **Malvolio**. There's no anger in this speech at all.

At the beginning, pick up the ring before you start and be genuinely puzzled. It soon dawns on **Viola** that **Olivia** is attracted to her – a thought which she might find lightly amusing – but then she makes a great leap forward with the sudden insight 'She loves me, sure'. This takes her aback, she thinks through the situation and realises the truth - '..... I am the man'!

Now a change in tone and we see **Viola's** compassion.

Poor lady, she were better love a dream!

She doesn't say 'Foolish lady', she says 'Poor lady' and it works well if the actor speaks this with sincerity. **Viola** is perhaps experiencing a fellow feeling with **Olivia** – she herself is nursing a seemingly hopeless love for **Orsino**.

The next six lines are tender – not only sympathetic to **Olivia** but to all women.

Disguise, I see thou art a wickedness
Wherein the pregnant enemy does much.
How easy is it for the proper-false

In women's waxen hearts to set their forms!
Alas, our frailty is the cause, not we,
For such as we are made of, such we be.

There is then a change of tone with the more mundane 'How will this fadge?' (turn out) and a quick summary of the plot, in which she allows herself some appealing self mockery when she describes herself as 'poor monster' *ie* neither man nor woman.

How will this fadge? My master loves her dearly,
And I, poor monster, fond as much on him,
And she, mistaken, seems to dote on me.
What will become of this? As I am man,
My state is desperate for my master's love.
As I am woman, now, alas the day,

This section ends with another expression of sympathy for **Olivia.**

What thriftless sighs shall poor Olivia breathe!

She has now thought through the situation and being a practical girl, decides she can't do anything about it, so speaks the final rhyming couplet quite jauntily,

O time, thou must untangle this, not I.
It is too hard a knot for me t'untie.

perhaps puts the ring in her pocket and exits. (I've seen an actor throw the ring in the air at the end of the couplet and catch it and it worked well).

Moves are not required throughout this speech – just face front and share your thoughts with your audience. A manly stride as you exit would remind us of what **Viola** is pretending to be and would give an amusing finish to the scene.

'Made good view of me' means examined me closely, 'proper-false' means handsome deceiver and 'the pregnant enemy' is Satan.

BOTTOM

A Midsummer Night's Dream act 4 scene 1

Bottom is a weaver, a working man, ostensibly from Athens, but clearly in Shakespeare's mind he comes from deepest Warwickshire. Some sort of regional accent then is required. He is referred to in the text as 'bully Bottom', which can lead the actor astray. He's not a bully – bully in Shakespeare's day meant 'fine fellow', a friend – the life and soul of the party if you like and that's what **Bottom** certainly is.

He and his friends, who are also working men of different trades, are rehearsing a play called 'Pyramus and Thisbe' and **Bottom** is in his element. He LOVES acting, and he never gives half measures. He adores entering a romantic world where valiant heroes rescue damsels in distress. Who better to play **Pyramus**, who slays the lion that threatens the fair **Thisbe**, than he? He thinks he'd be wonderful as the lion too. (Not TOO terrifying of course, in case the ladies in the audience should take fright – no, he would 'roar as gently as any sucking dove').

He has a powerful imagination: he never notices the glaring shortcomings of the amateur production which he and his homespun friends are preparing for **Duke Theseus** on his wedding day – to him it's all GLORIOUS.

What he DOES notice is that the heroine, **Thisbe**, is rather a good part too – so maybe some way could be found for him to play ALL THREE! Oh, and if there's a TYRANT in the play, he could play ALL FOUR!! He's TERRIFIC at tyrants – they are parts 'to tear a cat in'.

He's finally persuaded by **Peter Quince** to stick to **Pyramus**. 'You can play no part but Pyramus: for Pryamus is a sweet-faced man; a proper man as one shall see in a summer's day; a most lovely, gentleman-like man: therefore you must needs play Pyramus'. This deft flattery finds its mark and **Bottom** graciously consents to confine himself to just the one part. **Pyramus** is, after all, THE HERO.

And now, exciting decisions must be made 'What beard would I best to play it in? (He's obviously got a large collection at home).

He soon gets rather more than a beard – **Puck**, the 'knavish sprite', who works for **Oberon** (King of the

Fairies), watching the workmen rehearsing, decides (unkindly) that **Bottom** is an ass and 'transforms' him by replacing his head with that of a donkey's.

Titania (Queen of the Fairies), who has been sleeping nearby, wakes up from a drugged sleep and falls instantly in love with him – she 'straightway loved an ass'. Their courtship is immediate but tender. Fairies are summoned to attend on him and all manner of comforts are provided. He eventually falls into a deep and contented sleep by **Titania's** side.

Oberon then takes pity on **Titania** for the trick he has played on her – it was he who ordered **Puck** to 'streak her eyes' with the juice of a magic purple flower, which made her fall in love with **Bottom**. He releases her from the spell, the asses head is removed from **Bottom**, who is still sleeping and he is left alone.

He wakes.

When my cue comes, call me and I will answer. My next is 'most fair Pyramus'. Heigh-ho. Peter Quince? Flute the bellows-mender? Snout the tinker? Starveling? God's my life! Stolen hence, and left me asleep? – I have had a most rare vision. I have had a dream past the wit of man to say what dream it was. Man is but an ass if he go about t'expound this dream. Methought I was – there is no man can tell what. Methought I was – and methought I had – but man is but a patched fool if he will offer to say what methought I had. The eye of man hath not heard, the ear of man hath not seen, man's hand is not able to taste, his tongue to conceive, nor his heart to report, what my dream was. I will get Peter Quince to write a ballad of this dream. It shall be called 'Bottom's Dream', because it hath no bottom; and I will sing it in the latter end of a play, before the Duke. Peradventure, to make it the more gracious, I shall sing it at her death.

The actor might well lie snoring for a few seconds before waking – a good effect if the snores sound rather like a donkey. **Bottom** is in a dreamlike state, halfway between man and donkey.

Initially, he thinks he's still in rehearsal, so his first line is said matter-of-factly to his companions and he reminds them of his next cue.

When my cue comes, call me and I will answer.
My next is 'most fair Pyramus'.

He might still have his eyes shut before waking himself with a full-scale donkey bray immediately before 'Heigh-ho!' (It's a broad comic effect and it works).

When he calls for his companions, call loudly as if hoping for an answer.

Peter Quince? Flute the bellows-mender? Snout the tinker? Starveling?

When none comes, you might put your hand on your head as if you sensed there was something different about it – and then some vague memory of the time with **Titania** comes flooding back.

Say

I have had a most rare vision. I have had a dream past the wit of man to say what dream it was.

Slowly and with great wonder.

Be unconscious of the humour in 'Man is but an ass' – **Bottom** has no inkling that his predicament is amusing. To him, his experience has been the stuff of legends – he is the hero in an epic saga, even grander than the one he's been rehearsing. It's all VERY serious for him and he has no idea when he says

The eye of man hath not heard, the ear of man hath not seen, man's hand is not able to taste, his tongue to conceive, nor his heart to report, ...

that he may not be expressing himself quite as eloquently as he thinks. He is half remembering the phrase 'Eye hath not seen, nor ear heard .... ' Chapter 2 verse 9, 1 Corinthians from the Bible which he would (no doubt) have heard in his regular devout churchgoing - and he misremembers it.

He then suddenly, has a wonderful idea – he will get **Peter Quince** to write a HIT SONG about his dream – so the whole WORLD will know.

I will get Peter Quince to write a ballad of this dream.

Even better, the song will have HIS NAME in its title.

It shall be called 'Bottom's Dream',

Shakespeare then reminds us that **Bottom** is not fully free from his dreamlike state when he says

I will sing it in the latter end of a play,

It's clearly the play he's been rehearsing, but he seems detached from it. Then he remembers the Duke and his mind clears.

...... before the Duke.

He has one last fabulous idea – he'll sing it when Thisbe DIES.

Peradventure, to make it the more gracious, I shall sing it at her death.

His theatrical juices are flowing again and he can't wait to rush to rehearsals. He might just touch his head once more, in slight puzzlement, before running off to meet his friends.

This is a speech which is touching and funny all at the same time. It is ten times more effective when acted than read. Remember Shakespeare wrote for actors and respected their art.

'Patched' refers to the parti-coloured costume worn by medieval fools – who were entertainers. 'Peradventure' means perhaps.

GONERIL

Lear has abdicated from the Throne and given his realm to his two deceitful eldest daughters, **Goneril** and **Regan**. He would have included his youngest daughter, **Cordelia**, but she didn't flatter him enough, so has been denied her share. He then decides to live alternately with **Goneril** and **Regan,** who soon show their true colours. They are deeply irritated by their irascible old father, who insists on carrying on just as if he were still King, arriving at their palaces with a huge retinue of insolent and riotous knights.

Goneril confronts her father and he pretends that he doesn't know her name.

This is her reply:

> *This admiration, sir, is much of the savour*
> *Of other your new pranks. I do beseech you*
> *To understand my purposes aright:*
> *As you are old and reverend, you should be wise.*
> *Here do you keep a hundred knights and squires;*
> *Men so disorder'd, so debauched and bold,*
> *That this our court, infected with their manners,*

Shows like a riotous inn. Epicurism and lust
Make it more like a tavern or a brothel
Than a graced palace. The shame itself doth speak
For instant remedy. Be then desired,
By her that else will take the thing she begs,
A little to disquantity your train,
And the remainder that shall still depend
To be such men as may besort your age,
Which know themselves and you.

This speech is a good choice for an actor with personal authority, who is good at icy disdain. **Goneril** speaks to her ancient father like a sarcastic schoolmistress chastising an errant schoolboy. She refers to his 'pranks' and reminds him that at his age, 'he SHOULD be wise'.

It's an imperious speech, delivered through (metaphorically) clenched teeth. The actor might well take the natural pitch of her voice up a notch. She is very angry indeed, but she remains physically poised and never loses her temper. The anger is always in control.

Stress the consonants throughout and stand tall.

'Admiration' means astonishment, 'shows' means appears, 'epicurism' is luxurious success, 'disquantity' means reduce, 'besort' means be suitable, 'know themselves and you' means know their place and behave in a way fitting for your service.

PROTEUS

The Two Gentlemen of Verona act 2 scene 4

'Protean' means changeable – it comes from the name of the Grecian sea-god, Proteus, who could change his shape at will. Our **Proteus** then is aptly named.

The background is this:

Proteus has a faithful girlfriend, his 'heavenly **Julia**', who he's mad about. His bosom buddy, **Valentine** (the other of the Two Gentlemen) also has a girlfriend who HE'S mad about – the newly acquired and beauteous **Sylvia**. All is well until **Proteus** meets her (when he says "tis but her picture I have yet beheld', he means he's been dazzled by her outward appearance, not that he has only seen a likeness of her in a portrait – he has actually just spoken to her). He's immediately smitten and poor **Julia** is quickly forgotten. For **Proteus**, it's passion at first sight.

> *Even as one heat another heat expels,*
> *Or, as one nail by strength drives out another,*
> *So the remembrance of my former love*
> *Is by a newer object quite forgotten.*

Is it mine eye, or Valentine's praise,

Her true perfection, or my false transgression

That makes me, reasonless, to reason thus?

She is fair, and so is Julia that I love –

That I did love, for now my love is thawed,

Which like a waxen image 'gainst a fire

Bears no impression of the thing it was.

Methinks my zeal to Valentine is cold,

And that I love him not as I was wont.

O, but I love his lady too-too much,

And that's the reason I love him so little.

How shall I dote on her with more advice,

That thus without advice begin to love her?

'Tis but her picture I have yet beheld,

And that hath dazzled my reason's light.

But when I look on her perfections

There is no reason but I shall be blind.

If I can check my erring love I will,

If not, to compass her I'll use my skill.

There's a bold directness about this speech, so plunge straight in. Be a bit of a 'Jack-the-lad' (a brash, self-assured young man) – when **Proteus** sees something he wants he goes straight for it. He's young and lusty and he's out for a good time. Any pangs of guilt about betraying **Julia** and

Valentine are swiftly brushed aside.

Go for comedy on the flippant lines

Methinks my zeal to Valentine is cold,
And that I love him not as I was wont.
O, but I love his lady too-too much,
And that's the reason I love him so little.

Be cool, witty and cynical – easy with yourself and with the audience. Stand still, feet apart – a confident stance. Be likeable and cheeky. Look as though you are enjoying yourself. There's an underlying excitement in everything you say – make us share that excitement.

By 'reasonless' he means he's been blown out of his mind by the sight of the girl. 'Advice' means consideration and 'compass' means possess.

82

YOURSELF

Shall I compare thee to a summer's day?
Thou art more lovely and more temperate:
Rough winds do shake the darling buds of May,
And summer's lease hath all too short a date:
Sometime too hot the eye of heaven shines,
And often is his gold complexion dimmed;
And every fair from fair sometime declines,
By chance or nature's changing course untrimmed;
But thy eternal summer shall not fade,
Nor lose possession of that fair thou ow'st,
Nor shall death brag thou wander'st in his shade,
When in eternal lines to time thou grow'st;
So long as men can breathe or eyes can see,
So long lives this, and this gives life to thee.

Yes, the character who is speaking is yourself. You are talking to someone you love. If there is no one suitable in your life, then think of a film actor or pop star who has taken your fancy – it helps to have someone definite in mind.

You've been thinking of all the wonderful things that your loved one reminds you of. A beautiful piece of music perhaps, a dancer's graceful movement, a great painting, or even your favourite meal ('I could EAT you'). Eventually you decide on 'a summer's day' but you immediately think it's not such a good idea because nothing fits. You find plenty of reasons why and go through a list of them.

By the time you get to the line 'But thy eternal summer shall not fade', you've definitely decided it's a ROTTEN idea, but you haven't wasted your time because it dawns on you that if you write it down, you will have written something which could be around for a long, long time – long after you and your loved one have died. And, if you manage to get it published, then people could go on reading it FOREVER.

Be aware of the form of your sonnet: the usual fourteen lines, with an alternate rhyme scheme in the first twelve, followed by the confident and conclusive final rhyming couplet (Shakespeare's sonnets – English sonnets - comprise of three stanzas of four lines with alternate rhymes and a couplet rhymed and there are ten syllables per line).

It's an elegant kind of writing, very concentrated, so it needs to be performed with care and precision.

Clarity is vital, so make sure that you are absolutely certain of the meaning of each phrase. Give your performance momentum by stressing the second half of each line, using an upward inflection at the end of each line. Observe the punctuation, but keep it moving along.

It's a good idea to have a sonnet in reserve whenever you audition. Time may be at a premium for some reason or other and you will have your short piece ready.

It's also a wonderful self-discipline to perform a sonnet – you can't hide behind a character, or dash about gesturing – you have to be very clear, very simple and very sincere. In other words, you have to employ in a distilled version, all the qualities you need to bring to any Shakespearean speech.

Shakespeare didn't write his sonnets to be performed. I don't think he'd mind though, provided they are performed well.

LINE LEARNING

1   Learn your lines as soon as possible: don't put it off. It is only when you have thoroughly learnt them that you will be comfortable in **acting** them. Actors learn lines in different ways – some by recording them on tape and playing it back to themselves, others by covering the speech with a postcard and going down the lines, only checking when they are uncertain of the next word. I favour the latter – listening to yourself can be a dreadful 'put off' – you will start criticising your performance and it's too early to do that.

2   You may find it useful to learn your lines last thing at night, close the book, then go to sleep. On waking, you may find that you seem to know them.

3   Get your family or a friend to 'hear' you as many times as you can. Speak them out good and loud and in the early stages, act them in different ways, not sticking to the same stresses.

4   Work out exactly where you are going to take breaths – usually on a full stop, comma,

exclamation or question mark – never at the end of a line with no punctuation (a run-on line). Stick to your plan, use your full lung capacity, speaking as many lines as you can on one breath.

5   Learn the words so thoroughly that even if your concentration wavers, they will still keep coming. A performance of any nature is subject to many distractions. You can't stop acting and say 'I can't go on, it's too noisy here' or complain that your audience is not reacting to your lines in the way you would wish. Audiences, whether they are one person or 3000, are always unpredictable – that's what makes live acting so exciting.

6   It is only when you have learned your lines thoroughly that you can truly 'inhabit' them and fully identify with the character. Perhaps that's why it's called 'learning by **heart**' and not 'learning by **head**'.

HOW FREE CAN I BE IN MY CHOICE OF SPEECHES?

It depends on who you are auditioning for. If it's for a Drama School, then you may have to learn the speeches which they suggest. Some, like the Royal Academy of Dramatic Art in London, leave the choice to you but send out a list of the famous speeches which they DON'T want to hear because they have heard them too often before.

My own feeling is that a famous speech is popular because it's good and gives plenty of opportunities to the actor, so I don't mind hearing it again and again. It's always interesting to see the variety of valid interpretations which different actors can bring to it.

However, if you are asked to avoid certain speeches, then you would be foolish to ignore instructions – a Drama School is unlikely to look favourably on an actor who disobeys instructions even before s/he has joined the 'firm', no matter how talented.

In drama examinations, such as those of Trinity College, there are no restrictions except those of time. The length of time allowed for each grade of examination is clearly printed in the syllabus. A little 'under' is fine, but never go over.

The Examiner would be very loath to stop you in mid-flow, but if you go way over your time s/he may have to stop you in the interests of fairness to others and keeping to the timetable.

I'm always surprised that actors seem to feel so bound by their gender – Shakespeare's own company certainly wasn't. In his day, all the female parts were played by boys. There were no female actors on the English stage until 1660 – forty-four years after Shakespeare's death.

The first **Juliet, Lady Macbeth, Rosalind, Ophelia, Viola, Portia, Isabella, Titania, Beatrice, Cleopatra, Imogen** and a host of others, were all played by boys. They must have been brilliant, or Shakespeare wouldn't have written such wonderful parts for them.

So, if any boy is courageous enough to take on one of these roles, he is in a great tradition which has continued intermittently until the present day. Mark Rylance, who runs Shakespeare's Globe Theatre in London, has recently given us a notable **Cleopatra** and a strikingly original **Olivia** in **Twelfth Night**.

There was also a splendid all male production of **As You Like It** at Sir Laurence Olivier's National Theatre in the late 60's, when Anthony Hopkins (not yet 'Sir' and now more famous for playing Hannibal Lecter) gave us a riotous **Audrey**, complete with blond plaits.

Olivier himself was talent spotted by the great actress Dame Sybil Thorndike, when he played **Katherine** in **The Taming of the Shrew** in a school production and recently Adrian Lester, who is both male and black, was a celebrated **Rosalind**.

It works the other way too – I have in my possession a print of Miss Ellen Bateman as **Richard III**, a part she played in 1851 (apparently to great effect) at the age of SEVEN. What a trouper she must have been. She glowers at the onlooker with a chilling malevolence, aided by a tiny Hitler-style moustache.

At about the same time, Miss Charlotte Cushman, the American actress, was intriguing audiences with her **Romeo** (to her sister's **Juliet**), her **Hamlet** and her **Oberon**.

In the late 19th century the flamboyant French

actress, Sarah Bernhardt, stormed through the role of **Hamlet** with her usual flair and to tumultuous applause. She never lost her splendid panache, on or off stage, even after the amputation of a leg.

Nearer our own time, Dame Sybil, already mentioned, spotted an opportunity during the First World War, when many young actors were away on active service. She dashed off a creditable **Prince Hal, Puck, Launcelot Gobbo** and **Ferdinand**.

Almost bang up to date, in the last decade, Fiona Shaw played **Richard II**, Frances de la Tour took possession of **Hamlet** and Vanessa Redgrave undertook the role of **Prospero**.

So, if you are female and want to have a go at any of the masculine roles, why not? There are plenty of splendid precedents and scores of wonderful parts to choose from.

But remember – it will be your PERFORMANCE which is assessed, not your choice of material.

HOW TO BEHAVE AT AUDITIONS

In a word, CHEERFULLY. Everyone knows that an audition is an ordeal and that however well prepared you are, you will experience heart sinking moments of panic and self-doubt. That is perfectly normal. The real test is how you deal with them.

If you are auditioning for a job, a place in a drama school, or a part in an amateur production, the person in charge of the audition will not just be looking for talent, they will be looking for someone who will 'fit in' and be a good colleague.

A cheerful person in other words, someone who is pleasant to be with.

Don't announce to the person taking the audition that you are nervous. There's little they can do except mouth useless platitudes like 'there's no need to be' or 'just relax and enjoy yourself' and it all wastes valuable time.

Pretend that you are NOT nervous – if you are a good actor, it might work. Be assured that everyone wants you to do well: they are on your side and they want to like you.

Similarly, if you are acting in a drama examination, the examiner will do his/her best to make you feel at ease and will be looking forward eagerly to your performance. No one wants to 'catch you out', they want to enjoy your work and celebrate what is good about it.

Any critical comments in your examination report will be there to help you improve – don't feel defensive about them – have the humility to acknowledge that they might just be right.

A LIST OF DOs AND DON'Ts

1 Arrive AT LEAST fifteen minutes before your appointment. I recommend at least half an hour – the car / bus / tube / train might be late. PUNCTUALITY is the number one rule in the theatre. Besides there may be a cancellation before your allotted time and you'll win points by being able to step into the breach.

2 Talk pleasantly to the other actors who may be waiting and be supportive – share the camaraderie of the waiting room.

3 Don't 'size them up' and think they must be better than you, because they look more confident or are taller / shorter / thinner / better looking etc. You won't know exactly what is being looked for and it might be a quality which only you have.

4 Try to avoid going through the words in your head – you may forget them and this will panic you. By now you will have reached a point where the words are associated with your moves and gestures and without those, the words may well float away.

5 A few minutes before you are 'on', calm yourself by breathing deeply through the nose and out through the mouth. Don't forget to yawn, which relaxes your vocal equipment.

6 When you enter the acting space, smile and greet the people who are waiting for you – have a general air of 'readiness'.

7 If you need a chair for your performance (and there is always a chair at an audition), don't ask if you can use it – just move it to where you want it to be. This will make you seem capable.

8 If you have a cold, or are not feeling well, don't mention it – it will sound like an excuse. The director/examiner can only go on what you bring to the audition, s/he can't assess what you might be like WITHOUT a cold or if you WERE feeling well. If your cold is obvious, s/he will be impressed that you didn't make a fuss and let it put you off. Being a trouper is highly valued in the theatre.

9   There is no need for an elaborate introduction to your piece – a short announcement will do. The chances are that the director/examiner will know the play anyway. However, be prepared to 'fill them in' if they ask.

10 If you forget your words in the first line or two, you may ask to start again. After that, try to keep going – think of something to say or cut to a line which you DO know. You will be admired for your quick thinking. At the end, you might say 'I got some of the words wrong, please forgive me'. You undoubtedly will be forgiven, far more than if you have limped along with a lot of prompting. Prompts are always bad news – belief flies out of the window – and in any case, who is going to prompt? The person auditioning you wants to look at YOU not at your script. And please don't say 'I knew it last night' – you can't really say that to an audience, can you?

11 When you have finished and you've received an indication that your time is over, say 'Thank you' and GO. Don't linger around hoping to be given an indication of your

result – you won't be. Besides, it's someone else's turn now – the timetable must be kept as a courtesy to them.

WHAT TO WEAR

Something comfortable, something you move in easily and which doesn't distract. Black is always a good choice – it's stylish and neutral – but otherwise, anything which gives a slight hint of the character you are playing is useful.

Don't wear something you have never worn before – it will worry you. If it IS new, be sure you have rehearsed in it. If you are playing a female part, wear a long practice skirt. It will help you to move correctly. (A full-scale production of Shakespeare may well be set in modern dress, but for auditions it is wiser to stick to the period).

Shoes should be flat or with a small heel. Those dearly loved trainers scream 21st century and they won't help you to feel right.

Even worse, and I've come across this, are huge platform shoes. A girl turned up to play St Joan at one of my auditions in four-inch versions, complete with shiny pink bows. I invited her to slip them off (barefoot is fine), but she loved them too much. I can't remember her performance, but I remember the shoes.

FINALLY

Spare a thought for the person auditioning you. It's not always plain sailing for them either – although it can be amusing.

I once auditioned a rather solemn young man who came in wearing a dark, formal suit, collar and tie and highly polished shoes. He'd chosen the madcap **Mercutio's** Queen Mab speech, from **Romeo and Juliet**. This seemed an odd choice for him, but of course, you never know.

I invited him to start. There was a pause as he looked gloomily round the room and said

'I can't see a stool.'
'Pardon?'
'A stool, I can't see one.'
'You need a stool?'
'Yes, about this high.' (He indicated approximately two feet).
'I'm afraid we don't have a stool – would this chair do?'
'No, it's got to be a stool.'
'But it's about the right height isn't it?'
'Yes, but it's not a stool.'
'Couldn't we PRETEND that it's a stool?'

'But it isn't.'

'Well, no, but YOU'RE not **Mercutio** but you're going to pretend you are – couldn't we extend that a bit and include the chair?'

'It's GOT to be a stool – I've REHEARSED with a stool!'

'Right, I understand, fine – well let's see what we can do.'

I hunted around amongst the lumber at the back of the rehearsal room and – miraculously – found one.

'Well, would you believe it – here's a stool.'

'It's not high enough.'

'Look, is it absolutely essential that you have a stool?'

'Yes, it is – it's a vital part of my performance.'

'What about this table?' (It was the one I'd been keeping all my papers on).

'How high is it?'

'Well, there it is – it looks about two and a half feet to me. What do you think?'

'It's a bit higher than a stool.'

'Yes, I suppose it is, but do you think you could possibly manage with it?'

'Well, it's not a stool, is it?'

'Not strictly speaking, no. But would you like to try it and see if it will do?'

'Oh, alright then.'

He then stood around while I dragged the table to the acting area and he indicated where I should put it. I think he felt too well-dressed for strenuous physical exertion.

'Is that about right?'

'I think so.'

'Good! Right! Splendid! Would you like to start?'

I went back to my seat and waited. Eventually, after contemplating the table for a while, he climbed onto it, immediately jumped off it, intoned the lines and never went near it again.

I hope you've enjoyed reading this book
And now, as Hamlet says
'GO MAKE YOU READY!'

SHAKESPEARE'S LIFE AND WORK

William Shakespeare was baptised on 26th April 1564 in Holy Trinity Church, Stratford on Avon. As this ceremony normally took place three days after the birth of a child, it is reasonable to assume that he was born on 23rd April, St George's day.

His father, John, was a prosperous glove maker and wool merchant who became Mayor of Stratford in 1568. His mother, Mary Arden, was the daughter of a local landowner.

William was the eldest of eight children – four boys and four girls – the youngest boy, Edmund, also became an actor and died at the age of twenty-seven.

William almost certainly attended Stratford's Grammar School, where he would have studied Latin, Mathematics, the Bible and Classical texts as well as 'Rhetoric' – speaking texts aloud with suitable expression and gestures. The latter would have stood him in good stead when he became an actor.

On leaving school, he may have worked for his

father, or he may have become a teacher – no one is certain – but we do know that at the age of eighteen he married Anne Hathaway, a farmer's daughter from nearby Shottery, who was eight years his senior and already pregnant with their first child.

Their daughter, Susannah, was born in May 1583, to be followed by twins, Hamnet and Judith, in 1585. Again, during this period we are not sure how Shakespeare was employed, but he may well have joined one of the acting companies (possibly Queen Elizabeth's Men), which came to Stratford at irregular intervals and would have been received by his father in his capacity as Bailiff of the town. Certainly by the time Hamnet died in 1596, aged 11, we know that Shakespeare was well established in London pursuing his theatrical career.

In 1594 he had joined a company of actors called, after their wealthy patron, The Lord Chamberlain's Men (re-named The King's Men in 1603 on the accession of James 1) and when The Globe Theatre was built in 1599, he was its resident playwright.

He also had another wealthy patron, Henry Wriothesley, the Earl of Southampton, to whom he dedicated two long poems, **Venus and Adonis** and **The Rape of Lucretia**, and who was the most likely recipient of the 154 sonnets which describe the emotional triangle between a poet, a young man and an older woman.

His early plays, dating from the late 1580s/early 1590s include **The Two Gentlemen of Verona, The Taming of the Shrew, Henry VI, Titus Andronicus** and **Richard III**. These established his fame and fortune.

With each succeeding play his characters grew in depth and subtlety – characters such as **Hamlet, Romeo, Shylock, Macbeth, Rosalind, Juliet, Benedick, Beatrice** and scores of others. Some of them seem as real to us as many of the people we meet and they have done for each succeeding generation.

A recent book by an American scholar, Harold Bloom, even suggests that Shakespeare 'invented personality'. That's a very large claim, but certainly Shakespeare was the first and greatest playwright who gave us characters who can be understood in terms of modern psychology.

Shakespeare wrote at the rate of approximately two plays a year. Towards the end of his career, he collaborated with other playwrights on **Henry VIII** and **The Two Noble Kinsmen**, but his final, unaided play, was **The Tempest**, which contains the memorable line *'Our revels now are ended.'*

He retired around 1611 to Stratford – a wealthy man. He died on his birthday in 1616 and was buried in Holy Trinity Church, the scene of his baptism fifty-two years earlier.

APPENDIX B

SOME ECCENTRIC THEORIES

Shakespeare did not attend university and this has given rise to claims that he was therefore not educated enough to have written his plays. There have been many bizarre suggestions as to their imagined authorship, usually centering on an assortment of aristocrats and even aspiring to royalty in the unlikely person of Queen Elizabeth 1.

The most tenacious claims, however, have been made for the lawyer, Sir Francis Bacon, and Shakespeare's contemporary playwright, the university educated Christopher Marlowe. W S Gilbert (of Gilbert & Sullivan fame) suggested wittily that the way to solve the Bacon suggestion was to dig up the bodies of Bacon and Shakespeare and get Sir Herbert Beerbohm Tree (a flamboyant Edwardian actor) to recite 'To be or not to be' over the bodies – the one who turned over would be the author.

Bacon's candidature has lost support in modern times (if you read his writings you will easily see why) but the Marlowe suggestion is still alive and kicking.

I remember, only a couple of years ago, attending a lecture on the subject at St Nicholas' Church, Deptford, in London, where Marlowe was buried after he'd been stabbed to death in a tavern brawl in 1593.

The lecturer insisted that Marlowe wasn't buried there at all, that he hadn't even been murdered but he'd been spirited over to the Continent where he'd 'written all of Shakespeare's plays'. The lecturer offered as proof of this that 'none of Shakespeare's contemporaries had ever referred to him in writing'.

I rather unsportingly quoted various documented examples to the contrary, including the well known poem on his friend Shakespeare by Ben Jonson, which graced the first published edition of the complete works. This did not impress, however. Jonson's poem was dismissed as 'cryptic' and I was told sternly that if I studied the poem carefully I would find enough letters in it to make up the name 'c-h-r-i-s-t-o-p-h-e-r-m-a-r-l-o-w-e'.

This kind of dottiness is fairly common on the outer fringes of Shakespearean scholarship. It springs from a love of mystery, a passion for intrigue and an understandable bewilderment in the face of genius.

People seem to want to OWN Shakespeare and it's perfectly true that if you have played **Hamlet**, for instance, you feel that you have formed a direct link with the author.

I felt this myself and I also felt it when I played **Macbeth**. We toured many countries, including Iraq, and in Baghdad an Arab professor came round to my dressing room in a state of high excitement, telling me that the author MUST have been an Arab. I asked him why and he replied 'He THINKS like an Arab – and look at his name – SHEIKH Speare!' He meant it – he wanted to own Shakespeare too.

My own favourite theory concerning the authorship of the plays is that if they WEREN'T written by William Shakespeare, then they were written by someone else of THE SAME NAME.

APPENDIX C

WHERE TO GO FOR MORE HELP

If you are intrigued by the authorship question there are two fascinating books to challenge and haunt you. They are: **Shakespeare: New Evidence** by A D Wraight (*Adam Hart*) and **Who Wrote Shakespeare?** by John Michael (*Thames and Hudson*).

If you need help in understanding Shakespeare's texts and concerns you will find the *Palgrave Macmillan* **Masterguide Series** or the *Hodder and Stoughton* **Spotlight on Shakespeare Series** very useful. John Peck and Martin Coyle's **How to Study a Shakespeare Play** (*Palgrave Macmillan*) provides a great deal of support for students.

The most recent practical guide to the speaking of Shakespeare is **Speaking Shakespeare** by Patsy Rodenburg (*Methuen*) and the London College of Music and Media produce an excellent cassette **Speaking and Acting Shakespeare** that can be ordered from *LCM Publications*, Thames Valley University, St Mary's Road, London W5 5RF, UK.

One of the most daring of modern directors, Charles Marowitz, has written an intriguing account of his work in **Recycling Shakespeare** published by Methuen.

More is probably written on Shakespeare than any other playwright and it can be confusing to try to keep up to date. You or your teacher/tutor will always find the latest books reviewed in **Express** published by Trinity College, *London* and **Speech and Drama** published by the Society of Teachers of Speech and Drama.

APPENDIX D

SUGGESTED FURTHER READING

On Acting	Laurence Olivier *(Weidenfield & Nicolson)*
Playing Shakespeare	John Barton *(Methuen)*
Voice and the Actor	Cecily Berry *(Harrap)*
William Shakespeare, a Life	A L Rowse *(Macmillan)*
Prefaces to Shakespeare	H Granville Barker *(Princeton University Press)*
Shaw on Shakespeare	Ed. Edwin Wilson *(Cassell)*
Shakespeare the Player	John Southworth *(Sutton)*

ADDITIONAL TITLES AVAILABLE

All books may be ordered direct from:

DRAMATIC LINES   PO BOX 201   TWICKENHAM   TW2 5RQ   ENGLAND

freefone: 0800 5429570
t: 020 8296 9503
f: 020 8296 9503
e: mail@dramaticlinespublishers.co.uk
www.dramaticlines.co.uk

MONOLOGUES

THE SIEVE
AND OTHER SCENES
Heather Stephens
ISBN 0 9522224 0 X

The Sieve contains unusual short original monologues valid for junior acting examinations. The material in The Sieve has proved popular with winning entries worldwide in drama festival competitions. Although these monologues were originally written for the 8-14 year age range they have been used by adult actors for audition and performance pieces. Each monologue is seen through the eyes of a young person with varied subject matter including tough social issues such as fear, 'Television Spinechiller', senile dementia , 'Seen Through a Glass Darkly' and withdrawal from the world in 'The Sieve'. Other pieces include: 'A Game of Chicken', 'The Present', 'Balloon Race' and a widely used new adaptation of Hans Christian Andersen's 'The Little Match Girl' in monologue form.

CABBAGE
AND OTHER SCENES
Heather Stephens
ISBN 0 9522224 5 0

Following the success of The Sieve, Heather Stephens has written an additional book of monologues with thought provoking and layered subject matter valid for junior acting examinations. The Cabbage monologues were originally written for the 8-14 year age range but have been used by adult actors for audition and performance pieces.   The Aberfan slag heap disaster issues are graphically confronted in 'Aberfan Prophecy' and 'The Surviving Twin' whilst humorous perceptions of life are observed by young people in 'The Tap Dancer' and 'Cabbage'. Other pieces include: 'The Dinner Party Guest', 'Nine Lives' and a new adaptation of Robert Browning's 'The Pied Piper' seen through the eyes of the crippled child.

ALONE IN MY ROOM
ORIGINAL MONOLOGUES

Ken Pickering
ISBN 0 9537770 0 6

This collection of short original monologues includes extracts from the author's longer works in addition to the classics. Provocative issues such as poverty and land abuse are explored in 'One Child at a Time', 'The Young Person Talks' and 'Turtle Island' with adaptations from 'Jane Eyre', Gulliver's Travels' and 'Oliver Twist' and well loved authors include Dostoyevsky. These monologues have a wide variety of applications including syllabus recommendation for various acting examinations. Each monologue has a brief background description and acting notes.

DUOLOGUES

PEARS

Heather Stephens
ISBN 0 9522224 6 9

These thought provoking and unusual short original duologues provide new material for speech and drama festival candidates in the 8-14 year age range. The scenes have also been widely used for junior acting examinations and in a variety of school situations and theatrical applications. Challenging topics in Pears include the emotive issues of child migration, 'Blondie', 'The Outback Institution' and bullying 'Bullies', other scenes examine friendship, 'The Best of Friends', 'The Row' and envy, 'Never the Bridesmaid'. New adaptations of part scenes from 'Peace' by Aristophanes and 'Oliver Twist' by Charles Dickens are also included.

TOGETHER NOW
ORIGINAL DUOLOGUES

Ken Pickering
ISBN 0 9537770 1 4

This collection of short duologues includes extracts from Ken Pickering's longer works together with new original pieces. The variety of experiences explored in the scenes can all be easily identified with, such as an awkward situation, 'You Tell Her', and the journey of self knowledge in 'Gilgamesh', whilst 'Mobile phones', 'Sales' and 'Food' observe realistic situations in an interesting and perceptive way. Other duologues based on well known stories include 'Snow White' and 'The Pilgrim's Progress'. Each piece has a brief background description and acting notes. The scenes have syllabus recommendation for a number of examination boards and wide variety of theatrical and school applications.

SHAKESPEARE THE REWRITES
Claire Jones
ISBN 0 9522224 8 5

A collection of short monologues and duologues for female players. The scenes are from rewrites of Shakespeare plays from 1670 to the present day written by authors seeking to embellish original texts for performances, to add prequels or sequels or satisfy their own very personal ideas about production. This material is fresh and unusual and will provide exciting new audition and examination material. Comparisons with the original Shakespeare text are fascinating and this book will provide a useful contribution to Theatre Study work from GCSE to beyond 'A' level. Contributors include James Thurber (Macbeth) Arnold Wesker (Merchant of Venice) and Peter Ustinov (Romanoff and Juliet). The collection also includes a most unusual Japanese version of Hamlet.

RESOURCES

DRAMA LESSONS IN ACTION
Antoinette Line
ISBN 0 9522224 2 6

Resource material suitable for classroom and assembly use for teachers of junior and secondary age pupils. Lessons are taught through improvisation, these are not presented as 'model lessons' but provide ideas for adaptation and further development. Lessons include warm-up and speech exercises and many themes are developed through feelings such as timidity, resentfulness, sensitivity and suspicion. Material can be used by groups of varying sizes and pupils are asked to respond to texts from a diverse selection of well known authors including: Roald Dahl, Ogden Nash, John Betjeman, Ted Hughes, Michael Rosen, and Oscar Wilde.

AAARGH TO ZIZZ
135 DRAMA GAMES
Graeme Talboys
ISBN 0 9537770 5 7

This valuable resource material has been created by a drama teacher and used mostly in formal drama lessons but also in informal situations such as clubs and parties. The games are extremely flexible, from warm up to cool down, inspiration to conclusion and from deadly serious to purest fun and the wide variety ranges from laughing and rhythm activities to building a sentence and word association. Many games could be used as part of a PSHE programme together with activities connected with 'fair play'. The games are easily adapted and each has notes on setting up details of straightforward resources needed. All this material has been used with a wide range of young people in the 10 - 18 year age range.

DRAMA•DANCE•SINGING
TEACHER RESOURCE BOOK

edited by John Nicholas
ISBN 0 9537770 2 2

This collection of drama, dance and singing lesson activities has been drawn from a bank of ideas used by the Stagecoach Theatre Arts Schools teachers. Clearly presented lessons include speech and drama exercises, games and improvisations often developed as a response to emotions. Dance activities include warm-ups, basic dance positions, improvisations, versatile dance exercises and routines while singing activities help to develop rhythm and notation as well as providing enjoyable games to develop the voice. Activities can be easily adapted for large or small group use and are suitable for 6 - 16 year olds in a fun yet challenging way.

MUSICAL PLAYS

THREE CHEERS FOR MRS BUTLER   adapted by Vicky Ireland
ISBN 0 9537770 4 9

This versatile musical play about everyday school life is for anyone who has ever been to school. It features the poems and characters created by Allan Ahlberg with a foreword by Michael Rosen, songs by Colin Matthews and Steven Markwick and was first performed at the Polka Theatre for Children, London. The two acts of 40 minutes each can be performed by children, adults or a mixture of both and the play can be produced with a minimum cast of 7 or a large cast of any size, with or without music and songs, as well as having a wide variety of other musical and dramatic applications.

INTRODUCING OSCAR
The Selfish Giant & The Happy Prince

Veronica Bennetts
ISBN 0 9537770 3 0

Oscar Wilde's timeless stories for children have been chosen for adaptation because of the rich opportunities offered for imaginative exploration and the capacity to vividly illuminate many aspects of the human condition. The original dialogue, lyrics and music by Veronica Bennetts can be adapted and modified according to the needs of the pupils and individual schools or drama groups. The Selfish Giant runs for 25 minutes and The Happy Prince for 1 hour 15 minutes. Both musical can be used for Trinity College, *London.* examinations and are ideal for end of term productions, for drama groups and primary and secondary schools.

WHAT IS THE MATTER WITH MARY JANE?   Wendy Harmer
ISBN 0 9522224 4 2

This monodrama about a recovering anorexic and bulimic takes the audience into the painful reality of a young woman afflicted by eating disorders. The play is based on the personal experience of actress Sancia Robinson and has proved hugely popular in Australia. It is written with warmth and extraordinary honesty and the language, humour and style appeal to current youth culture. A study guide for teachers and students is included in this English edition ensuring that the material is ideal for use in the secondary school classroom and for PSHE studies, drama departments in schools and colleges in addition to amateur and professional performance.

X-STACY
Margery Forde
ISBN 0 9522224 9 3

Margery Forde's powerful play centres on the rave culture and illicit teenage drug use and asks tough questions about family, friends and mutual responsibilities. The play has proved hugely successful in Australia and this English edition is published with extensive teachers' notes by Helen Radian, Lecturer of Drama at Queensland University of Technology, to enrich its value for the secondary school classroom, PSHE studies, English and drama departments.

ASSEMBLIES! ASSEMBLIES! ASSEMBLIES!   Kryssy Hurley
ISBN 0 9537770 6 5

These teacher-led assemblies require minimum preparation and have been written by a practising teacher to involve small or large groups. Each assembly lasts 15-20 minutes and is suitable for Key Stages 2 and 3. There are 12 for each term and these explore many PSHE and Citizenship issues including bullying, racism, friendship, co-operation, feeling positive, making responsible choices and decisions, school rules and laws outside school. All have the following sections: *Resource and Organisation, What To Do, Reflection Time and Additional Resources and Activities.*

JELLY BEANS

Joseph McNair Stover
ISBN 0 9522224 7 7

The distinctive style and deceptively simple logic of American writer Joseph McNair Stover has universal appeal with scenes that vary in tone from whimsical to serious and focus on young peoples relationships in the contemporary world. The 10 to 15 minute original scenes for 2, 3, and 4 players are suitable for 11 year old students through to adult. Minimal use of sets and props makes Jelly Beans ideal for group acting examinations, classroom drama, assemblies, and a wide variety of additional theatrical applications.

SCENES 4 3 2 10 PLAYERS

Sandy Hill
ISBN 0 9537770 8 1

There are 10 original scenes in the book written for 3 to 10 players with opportunities for doubling-up of characters and introduction of optional additional players. The versatile scenes are of varying playing times and are suitable for performers from as young as 7 through to adult. The flexible use of sets and props have made these pieces particularly useful for group acting examinations and have proved to be immediately popular and successful for candidates as well as winning entries at drama festivals, they can also be used effectively for classroom drama and school assemblies. The scenes are often quirky and vary in tone with unusual endings. They will be enjoyed by performers and audiences alike.

WILL SHAKESPEARE SAVE US!
WILL SHAKESPEARE SAVE THE KING!

Paul Nimmo

ISBN 0 9522224 1 8

Two versatile plays in which famous speeches and scenes from Shakespeare are acted out as part of a comic story about a bored king and his troupe of players. These plays are suitable for the 11-18 year age range and have been produced with varying ages within the same cast and also performed by adults to a young audience. The plays can be produced as a double bill, alternatively each will stand on its own, performed by a minimum cast of 10 without a set, few props and modern dress or large cast, traditional set and costumes. The scripts are ideal for reading aloud by classes or groups and provide an excellent introduction to the works of Shakespeare. Both plays have been successfully performed on tour and at the Shakespeare's Globe in London.

SUGAR ON SUNDAYS
AND OTHER PLAYS

Andrew Gordon
ISBN 0 9522224 3 4

A collection of six one act plays bringing history alive through drama. History is viewed through the eyes of ordinary people and each play is packed with details about everyday life, important events and developments of the period. The plays can be used as classroom drama, for school performances and group acting examinations and also as shared texts for the literacy hour. The plays are suitable for children from Key Stage 2 upwards and are 40-50 minutes in length and explore Ancient Egypt, Ancient Greece, Anglo-Saxon and Viking Times, Victorian Britain and the Second World War. A glossary of key words helps to develop children's historical understanding of National Curriculum History Topics and the plays provide opportunities for children to enjoy role play and performance.

DRAMATIC LINES HANDBOOKS in association with
Trinity, The International Examinations Board

ACTING SHAKESPEARE FOR AUDITIONS AND EXAMINATIONS
ISBN 1 904557 10 4

Frank Barrie

☐

SPEECH AND DRAMA
ISBN 1 904557 15 5

Ann Jones and Bob Cheeseman

☐

THINKING ABOUT PLAYS
ISBN 1 904557 14 7

Giles Auckland-Lewis and Ken Pickering

☐

PREPARING FOR YOUR DIPLOMA IN DRAMA AND SPEECH
ISBN 1 904557 11 2

Ken Pickering and Kirsty N Findlay

☐

MUSICAL THEATRE
ISBN 1 904557 12 0

Gerry Tebbutt

☐

EFFECTIVE COMMUNICATION
ISBN 1 904557 13 9

John Caputo, Jo Palosaari and Ken Pickering